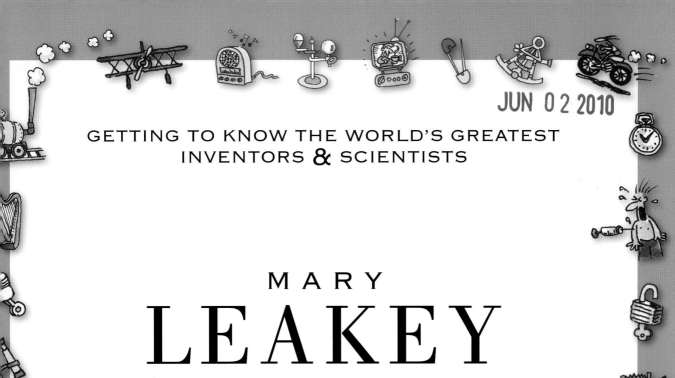

JUN 0 2 2010

GETTING TO KNOW THE WORLD'S GREATEST INVENTORS & SCIENTISTS

M A R Y
LEAKEY

Archaeologist Who Really Dug Her Work

F R I E N D S
OF THE MISSISSAUGA LIBRARY SYSTEM

Thank you for your
SUPPORT.

WRITTEN AND ILLUSTRATED BY MIKE VENEZIA

D1127627

CHILDREN'S PRESS®
AN IMPRINT OF SCHOLASTIC INC.
NEW YORK TORONTO LONDON AUCKLAND SYDNEY
MEXICO CITY NEW DELHI HONG KONG
DANBURY, CONNECTICUT

For Wende Fazio—thanks for being such an important part of my support team!

Reading Consultant: Nanci R. Vargus, Ed.D., Assistant Professor, School of Education,
University of Indianapolis

Content Consultant: Joyce Bedi, Senior Historian, Lemelson Center for the Study of Invention and
Innovation, National Museum of American History, Smithsonian Institution

Photographs © 2009: Art Resource, NY: 8 (Loïc Hamon/Réunion des Musées Nationaux), 4, 5 (Erich Lessing); Aurora
Photos/Bertrand Rieger/Hemis.fr: 9; Bridgeman Art Library International Ltd., London/New York: 11 (Erskine E. Nicol/Private
Collection/Chris Beetles, London, U.K.); Bruce Coleman Inc./Des & Jen Bartlett: 26; Corbis Images: 3, 28 (Bettmann), 20, 21
(Joe McDonald); National Geographic Image Collection: 31 (Kenneth Garrett), 24 (Melville B. Grosvenor); Photo Researchers,
NY/John Reader: 30; Photoshot/UPPA: 23; Royce Carlton, Inc.: 19 (by permission of Richard Leakey, from Adam's Ancestors,
by Louis Leakey, Harper Brothers, 1960); The Art Archive/Picture Desk: 16 (Gianni Dagli Orti/Musée des Antiquités Saint-
Germain-en-Laye); The Image Works/Topham: 18.

Colorist for illustrations: Andrew Day

Library of Congress Cataloging-in-Publication Data

Venezia, Mike.
   Mary Leakey : archaeologist who really dug her work / written and
illustrated by Mike Venezia.
      p. cm. — (Getting to know the world's greatest inventors and scientists)
   Includes index.
   ISBN-13: 978-0-531-23727-4 (lib. bdg.) 978-0-531-21336-0 (pbk.)
   ISBN-10: 0-531-23727-3 (lib. bdg.) 0-531-21336-6 (pbk.)
   1. Leakey, Mary D. (Mary Douglas) 1913–1996—Juvenile literature.
2. Women physical anthropologists—Tanzania—Biography—Juvenile
literature. 3. Women archaeologists—Tanzania—Biography—Juvenile
literature. 4. Fossil hominids—Tanzania—Olduvai Gorge—Juvenile
literature. 5. Olduvai Gorge (Tanzania)—Antiquities—Juvenile
literature. I. Title. II. Series.

   GN21.L372V46 2009
   301.092—dc22
   [B]
                                    2008027649

1 2 3 4 5 6 7 8 9 10 R 18 17 16 15 14 13 12 11 10 09

Mary and Louis Leakey studying fossils of human ancestors in Africa in 1959

Mary Nicol was born in London, England, in 1913. She became Mary Leakey when she married Louis Leakey in 1936. Both Louis and Mary became famous for their hunting skills. The Leakeys didn't hunt living animals, though. They were famous for hunting for human **fossils**, bones, and ancient tools.

Mary Leakey was always super-curious. This helped her to succeed in **archaeology** and **anthropology**. These two sciences deal with the study of our human **ancestors**.

Mary Leakey sought answers to an age-old question: where did humans come from? Almost every **culture** has a creation myth—a story of how humans came to be. This painting shows the Ancient Egyptians' story of how the world and humans were created.

They look at where humans came from, how they **evolved**, and how they lived thousands or even millions of years ago.

Ever since people first began walking the Earth, they probably wondered where they came from. Mary Leakey wanted to find out where we came from, too. Her discoveries helped answer parts of this fascinating question.

Mary Nicol had a very interesting and adventurous childhood. Her father, Erskine Nicol, was a successful artist. He supported his family by selling his paintings. He traveled all over Europe with his family, painting scenes of the countryside.

Mary's mother enjoyed painting, too, and didn't seem to mind traveling at all. When Mary was really little, she got used to having her "bedroom" set up on passenger trains. She slept on suitcases stacked between seats while traveling with her parents.

Mary didn't go to school while she was growing up. Her parents taught her math and reading and got her interested in archaeology.

Both Mr. and Mrs. Nicol loved to visit archaeological **excavations,** or digs. At one dig in France, after all the valuable **artifacts** had been removed, the director allowed Mary to sift through dirt and keep anything she found. Mary was thrilled! She found scrapers, flint blades, and parts of other tools made by humans thousands of years ago. Mary began to wonder exactly how long ago the tools had been made and who had made them. These scraps of tools were like treasures to Mary.

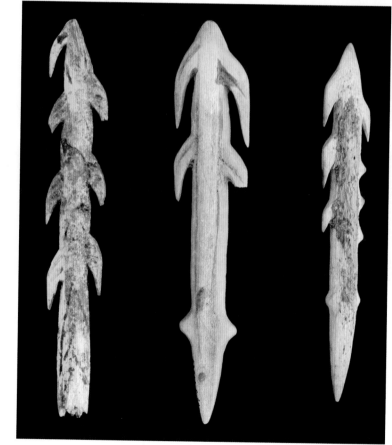

As a child, Mary was fascinated by the tools and fossils she saw while visiting archaeological digs in France. These 11,000-year-old **harpoons** are the types of tools she might have seen.

Mary's parents took her to see prehistoric cave paintings
very similar to these in Lascaux, France.

On one trip, Mary got the chance to explore
newly discovered caves that had Stone Age
paintings in them. Some of the paintings Mary
saw had been made over 15,000 years ago.

Sometimes, when cave openings were too small, Mr. Nicol refused to enter them. He was afraid of getting stuck. Mary and her mother would then go into the caves by themselves. Exploring caves was a magical experience that Mary never forgot.

When Mary was thirteen years old, a terrible thing happened. During a trip in France, Mr. Nicol became ill with cancer. He died a short time later. Mary was **devastated**. She and her mother returned to London, England. Mary stayed with her grandmother and aunts while her mother worked to sell Mr. Nicol's paintings. Selling the artwork was the only way Mrs. Nicols could earn enough money to support Mary and herself.

The Gamekeeper's Rest,
by Erskine E. Nicol

After raising enough money, Mary's mother decided it was finally time for her daughter to go to school. It didn't work out, though. Mary hated the idea of going to school. She did everything possible to get kicked out of two strict Catholic girl's schools. At one school, Mary faked having a fit by eating soap so that her mouth foamed up.

Then, in the science lab, she created a small explosion that upset everyone. Mary's mother tried to smooth things over, but it was too late. Mary was kicked out of school for good.

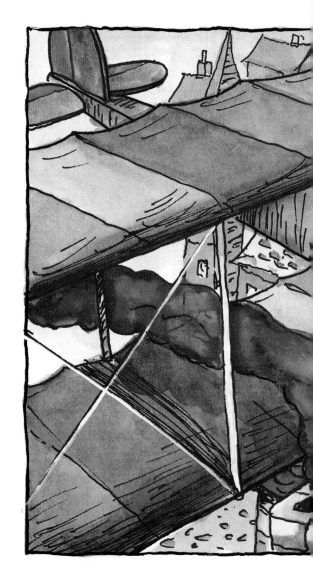

Now Mrs. Nicol was worried about her daughter's future. Mary wasn't worried, though. She knew there must be something she could do in the field of archaeology. Mary also thought she might try becoming an artist, like her father. Mary had begun drawing at an early age and was very good at it.

While deciding what to do with her future, Mary joined a gliding club. Being an adventurous

girl, Mary enjoyed the challenge of learning to become a glider pilot.

Once, Mary crashed her glider! Even though she wasn't hurt, she decided to give up her exciting hobby. Mary spent more time attending lectures on archaeology at a nearby university and at London's Natural History Museum.

Mary decided to see if she could help out on archaeological digs. She and her mother sent out letters to people leading some digs in England. In 1930, Mary was thrilled to be invited to assist at a few different excavations. While on the digs, she got important advice from professional archaeologists. She learned how to carefully scrape away thin layers of soil and spot any tiny particle that might be an ancient bone or tool fragment. Mary saw how experts patiently and skillfully **reconstructed** pieces of flint tools, bones, and pottery.

This is what an archaeological site looks like. Mary learned to sift through soil and rocks at sites like this to find fragments of ancient bones or tools.

Mary also put her drawing skills to use during this time. She drew pictures of the fossils and artifacts she found. Some of Mary's drawings were published in science articles. It wasn't long before other professional archaeologists became interested in Mary and her drawings.

Louis and Mary shared a love of discovery. This photograph shows them with a 1.7 million-year-old jaw and skull that Mary found in 1959. It was later discovered that this skull was an example of the oldest known human ancestor to use tools.

Soon Mary started being invited to attend archaeological **lectures** and events. At one dinner event, Mary was seated next to the world-famous anthropologist Louis Leakey. Even though Mary was just beginning her career, Louis took an interest in her.

He admired Mary's drawings and asked her to illustrate a new book he was writing. Before long, Mary and Louis realized they really liked each other. They enjoyed discussing anything having to do with archaeology.

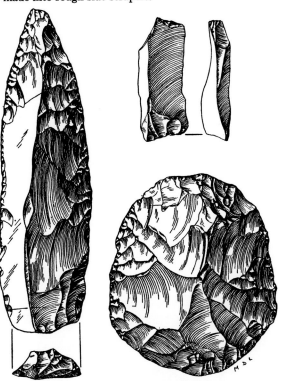

secondary flaking, in cases where the prepared flake that was knocked off the tortoise core did not come off quite in the shape that the maker intended. A few of the Levalloisian flakes, too, were made into rough side-scrapers.

Fig. 17.   Late Levalloisian tools and hand-axe
(reduced to about ⅔)

The early Levalloisian of Europe has a rather different distribution from that of the Middle Acheulean of the preceding interglacial or that of the Upper Acheulean of the next, or Riss-Würm interglacial, and it extends considerably farther to the north and east and much less to the south and west.

In the early 1930s, Mary drew illustrations for an archaeology book written by Louis Leakey. This is a page from that book showing one of Mary's illustrations of ancient tools. Her initials can be seen at the bottom right corner of the illustration.

At the time, Louis was no longer living with his first wife because the two of them had grown apart. She wanted to live in England, while he was happiest working on digs in Africa. They got a divorce in 1936. Later that year, Louis and Mary got married. It was the beginning of a remarkable period of scientific discovery for the two of them.

Mary fell in love with the beauty of East Africa.

Soon after the wedding, Louis and Mary headed off to Africa. Mary loved Africa. She was fascinated with the wild animals she saw there and could hardly believe the beauty of the vast land. Mary couldn't wait to start searching for fossils, ancient tools, and any other clues that would help her discover more about human history.

When Louis Leakey started his work, a lot of anthropologists believed that the earliest human beings began to show up on Earth in Europe or Asia. Louis always believed humans first appeared in the eastern part of Africa. Because of Louis and Mary Leakey's discoveries, most scientists today agree that human beings did begin in Africa. Over the years, Mary found pieces of humanlike bones that dated farther back in time than anyone could have imagined.

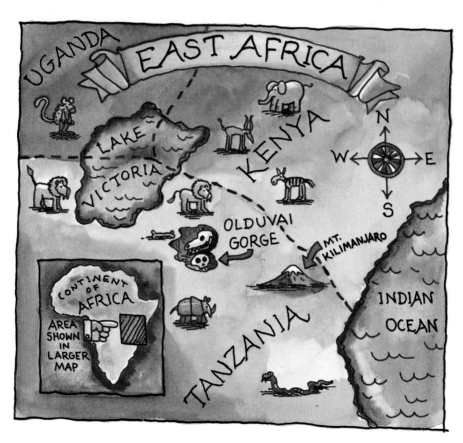

In 1948, Mary Leakey (at right) made an important discovery when she found a jaw and skull of *Proconsul*, an ancestor of both apes and early humans that lived millions of years ago.

In 1948, Mary found parts of a skull that were 18 million years old! Mary spent weeks carefully putting the pieces together. She discovered that the skull came from an apelike creature that was probably an ancestor of both apes and humans. She was the first person to find a fossil skull of this creature, named *Proconsul*. This discovery was an important clue in the search for early humans.

One of Mary and Louis's favorite places to hunt fossils was an area called the Olduvai Gorge, in what is now the African country of Tanzania. Over millions of years, the land of this area was covered with layers of dirt, rock, and volcanic ash. Then, earthquakes shifted the land, and

rivers washed away certain sections, leaving behind the 30-mile-long **ravine** that is there today. By looking at its walls, you can see the various layers of earth that have built up over time.

Olduvai Gorge, with its exposed layers of earth, was a wonderful place for Mary (at left) to hunt fossils.

Some different earth layers

Holocene
10,000 years ago

Pleistocene
1,800,000 years ago

Pliocene
5,300,000 years ago

Miocene
23,000,000 years ago

Oligocene
34,000,000 years ago

Eocene
54,000,000 years ago

One way scientists can tell a fossil's age is by looking at where the fossil is found in the earth's layers. Fossils in the upper layers, near the surface, can be thousands of years old. Those in the deeper layers may be millions of years old.

Mary (second from left) has a meal with her family while on a dig in Africa.

Mary made many important discoveries at Olduvai, including prehistoric fossils and tools that gave clues to how ancient peoples had lived. In 1959, Mary found skull pieces that were 1.75 million years old. Even though this skull wasn't as old as her first big discovery, it was more closely related to humans.

By this time, Mary and Louis had three sons. The boys—Jonathan, Richard, and Philip—spent their days working alongside their parents in the hot sun. They learned about archaeology and anthropology and made some important discoveries on their own.

Every time Mary and Louis Leakey made a new discovery they became more famous. Louis now spent most of his time traveling around the world giving lectures. Mary was happy to spend as much time as she could searching for fossils in and around the Olduvai Gorge.

Mary usually had one or more of her beloved Dalmatians at her side when she was working.

Mary felt right at home doing what she loved best. She often went to **remote** areas by herself. She always brought her pet Dalmatians along for protection.

In 1972, while preparing to give a lecture, Louis Leakey died of a heart attack. Now Mary was on her own. Without Louis, she continued her research in East Africa.

Mary Leakey examines the 3.6-million-year-old footprint trail she discovered at Laetoli, Tanzania.

A few years later, in 1978, Mary made her greatest discovery. In an area just south of the Olduvai Gorge, Mary discovered a remarkable set of fossilized footprints. They belonged to humanlike creatures who walked upright on two feet. Walking on two feet is a major thing that separates human beings from other **primates**. Mary could tell that the prints were left by a man, woman, and small child.

The footprints Mary found were more than 3.5 million years old. They were the oldest evidence of humanlike creatures ever found.

In 1983, 70-year-old Mary Leakey retired from **fieldwork**. She spent her time writing books and articles at her home in Nairobi, Kenya. By the time she died in 1996, Mary Leakey had become one of the most respected scientists in the world.

Mary displays a copy of the footprints from Laetoli.

Glossary

ancestor (AN-ses-tur) A relative who lived a long time ago

anthropology (an-thruh-POL-uh-jee) The study of the ways of life of people around the world

archaeology (ar-kee-OL-uh-jee) The excavation and study of ancient fossils and other artifacts to learn about the history of life on Earth

artifact (ART-uh-fact) An object made or changed by human beings

culture (KUHL-chur) A group of people who share customs and a way of life

devastated (DEV-uh-stay-tid) Very shocked and distressed

evolve (i-VOLV) To change slowly, over many thousands or millions of years

excavation (ek-skuh-VAY-shun) A place where archeaologists dig for ancient fossils and artifacts

fieldwork (FEELD-wurk) Work conducted by a researcher in the natural environment rather than in a laboratory

fossil (FOSS-uhl) The remains or traces of an animal or plant from millions of years ago, preserved as rock

harpoon (har-POON) A spearlike weapon attached to a rope and used to hunt whales or large fish

lecture (LEK-chur) A talk given to an audience in order to teach something

primate (PRYE-mate) Any member of the group of intelligent mammals that includes humans, apes, and monkeys

ravine (ruh-VEEN) A deep, narrow valley with steep sides

reconstruct (ree-kuhn-STRUHKT) To rebuild or piece together something that has been destroyed or broken

remote (ri-MOHT) Isolated or distant

Index